Macaron

Macaron

Alison Thompson

APPLE

Contents

Introduction

Crisp on the outside and soft in the middle, macarons are the favourite sweet treat of France. In essence, they consist of two slightly chewy, meringue-like 'shells', sandwiched together with rich buttercream or ganache. Nowadays, they are available in a seemingly infinite variety of colours and flavours.

Consisting of almond meal, icing sugar and egg whites, the macaron biscuit was originally created in Italy in 1533, and is thought to have made its way to France soon after. However, it wasn't until the beginning of the twentieth century that a pastry chef by the name of Pierre Desfontaines decided to join two macarons together with a flavoured ganache, to make the filled version we know today.

When making macarons, it is vital to use only the finest-quality ingredients. Correct technique is also essential in order to achieve the desired lightness, texture, sweetness and appearance. Biting into the perfect macaron, you should first experience a crisp shell-like exterior, then break through to a slightly chewy almond-meringue interior, and finish with a delicate, creamy filling.

Making macarons does require a little patience and practice, but if you take your time and follow the instructions carefully, you'll soon be baking macarons like a professional. Once you've mastered a few of the recipes in this book, try creating your own flavoured buttercreams, ganaches and jams using seasonal fruits, herbs or flavoured syrups – the possibilities are endless.

EQUIPMENT

Baking Trays - Flat baking trays are essential for achieving perfectly round macarons.

Double boiler - Used for melting chocolate, a double boiler consists of a saucepan one-third full of simmering water, with a heatproof bowl (larger than the pan) resting on top. The base of the bowl should not touch the water. (Alternatively, you can melt chocolate in the microwave, heating for 20 seconds at a time and stirring between bursts.)

Electric mixer - A free-standing electric mixer is ideal for making macarons, as lengthy periods of beating are required. However, a hand-held electric mixer can also be used. A whisk attachment is required for making the macaron shells and the buttercream fillings.

Piping nozzle - A plain (round) piping nozzle is used to pipe the macaron mixture onto the baking trays. I suggest using a 5-mm (¼-in) nozzle.

Piping bags - Disposable piping bags are the easiest and least messy product to use. A good alternative is a zip-lock bag with a small hole cut into one corner.

Sieve - A fine mesh sieve is essential for sifting dry ingredients such as flour, cocoa and icing sugar.

Sugar thermometer - A sugar or candy thermometer is needed to accurately measure the temperature of the sugar syrups used in the buttercreams.

INGREDIENTS

Almond meal (ground almonds) - Finely ground peeled almonds. (The more finely ground the almonds, the smoother your macaron shells will be.)

Chocolate - A ganache filling will only be as good as the quality of the chocolate used. Always use couverture chocolate, which contains a high cocoa butter content (32–39%). Some good brands include Lindt, Callebaut and Valrhona.

Cocoa - For best results, use a good-quality, unsweetened cocoa powder.

Crystallised violets - Organic violets that have been crystallised with sugar. Used as a garnish, they are available at specialty cooking stores.

Food colouring - Use gel food colourings, such as Wiltons or Squires. (Unlike more dilute colourings, they will not thin your mixture.) You need only a tiny amount to achieve vibrant colours. Available from specialty cooking stores and cake-decorating suppliers.

Gianduja - A sweet chocolate that contains about 30% hazelnut paste. Available at specialty cooking stores.

Griottine cherries - These morello cherries, macerated in kirsch, are a French delicacy. They are available at specialty cooking stores. If you can't find them, use canned morello cherries that have been drained then marinated in 2 tablespoons of kirsh for a couple of hours.

Hazelnut praline paste - A paste made from very finely ground hazelnuts and sugar. Available at specialty cooking stores.

Lavender - Dried lavender for use in cooking is available from specialty cooking stores. Fresh garden lavender may also be used, but only if it is organic.

Pistachio paste - A paste made from very finely ground pistachios and sugar, with green colouring added. Available at specialty cooking stores.

Rose extract - This concentrated rose flavouring is not to be confused with rosewater, which has a much more delicate flavour. Rosewater can be substituted for rose extract, but you'll need to multiply the quantity of extract specified in the recipe by four (e.g. 4 tablespoons rosewater is needed to replace 1 tablespoon rose extract). Rose extract is available at Indian and Middle Eastern grocers.

Saffron - Made from the dried stigma of the crocus flower, saffron adds a unique delicate flavour and brilliant yellow colour to foods. It can be purchased in thread or powder form. Beware imitations, which are made with artificial dyes and have no flavour.

Vanilla beans - Good-quality vanilla beans should be soft and supple. To remove the seeds, use a sharp knife to split the vanilla bean in half lengthways, then scrape out the seeds using the back of a small knife. Deseeded vanilla pods can be used to make vanilla sugar: simply bury the pods in a jar of sugar, leave for at least a week to allow the flavour to develop, then use the sugar for baking cakes, biscuits or slices.

Vanilla extract - A liquid concentrate made from vanilla beans. Be sure to use pure vanilla extract – vanilla essence is cheaper but contains artificial flavourings.

Violet extract - This concentrated violet flavouring can be found at specialty cooking stores or candy-making suppliers.

ESSENTIAL TECHNIQUES

Technique is very important if you want to create perfect macarons. Take your time practising the techniques and you will soon be achieving great results every time.

SIFTING THE DRY INGREDIENTS
Always sift the icing sugar and almond meal for the macaron shells twice. This process removes any larger lumps of almond meal, to ensure the shell forms a perfectly smooth dome when baked.

COLOURING THE SHELLS
When colouring macaron shells, add the food colouring to the egg whites towards the end of the beating process. The colour of the egg whites will resemble the colour of the baked shells.

MIXING THE SHELL MIXTURE
Once the almond meal and icing sugar have been added to the beaten egg whites, it is important to continue folding the mixture until it becomes glossy and moves slowly when the bowl is tilted. If you do not mix it to this stage the shells will not achieve a smooth dome when baked.

PIPING THE SHELLS
Ensure the baking trays are flat and the baking paper is lying flat on the tray. Pipe the rounds slightly smaller than required, as the mixture will spread a little after piping. Once the tray is filled, tap it firmly on the bench to remove any air bubbles from the mixture.

FORMING A CRUST

After piping the shells you must leave them to stand at room temperature until they form a crust. This will take 2–6 hours, depending on the temperature and humidity of the room. (The warmer and less humid the room, the faster the drying process.) When they are ready, you should be able to touch one lightly without any mixture sticking to your finger.

BAKING THE SHELLS

The oven temperatures provided in these recipes are for fan-forced ovens. If using an oven that is not fan-forced, you will need to set the dial 10–20°C (50–70°F) higher than the temperature specified. Every oven is different, so it may take a couple of tries before you find the perfect temperature for your oven. I recommend baking one tray of macaron shells at a time, until you find the right temperature. If the oven is too hot, the shells will crack and may also colour. If the oven is too cold, the shells will not rise and won't develop 'feet' (the ruffle or skirt around the base of the smooth shell), and they won't be cooked after the specified time.

MAKING FILLINGS

Macarons can be filled with ganache, buttercream or jam. For best results, use only the finest quality ingredients. For ganache fillings, take care not to overheat the chocolate when melting. When making buttercreams, make the sugar syrup in a small saucepan and use a sugar thermometer to accurately measure the temperature. Butter must be softened before use, so it can be easily incorporated.

STORING

Keep finished macarons refrigerated, in an airtight container, for up to 3 days. Always store them in single layers, between sheets of baking paper or foil – if stacked on top of each other they will stick together. Remove from the refrigerator 10 minutes before serving, to bring them to room temperature. Macarons can also be frozen, filled or unfilled, in an airtight container for up to 1 month.

The Perfect Macaron

♦♦♦ The shells should have a paper-thin crust enclosing the biscuity centre (the crust should not be crunchy).

♦♦♦ The surface of the shells should be completely smooth. (If the surface is bumpy, the almond meal has not been sifted well enough.)

♦♦♦ The texture of the interior of the shells should be light, soft and slightly chewy.

♦♦♦ The shells should have 'feet' around the base. (If these do not develop during baking, either the shells were not left to form a crust for long enough, or the oven temperature was too low.)

♦♦♦ The filling should be creamy, light and quite firm.

♦♦♦ The layer of filling should reach right to the edge of the shells, without being too thick: use too much filling and it will squash out the sides when you bite into the macaron; too little and you won't be able to taste it.

Basic
MACARON SHELLS

1. Line two baking trays with baking paper or silicon baking mats.

2. Combine the icing sugar and almond meal, and sift together twice, discarding anything remaining in the sieve. Set aside.

3. In the bowl of an electric mixer fitted with the whisk attachment, beat the egg whites on high speed until stiff peaks form. If colouring the macaron shell, add the food colouring to the egg whites now and beat in.

4. Fold the sifted sugar and almond meal into the egg whites, continuing to fold until the mixture is glossy and moves slowly when the bowl is tilted.

5. Spoon the mixture into a piping bag fitted with a 5-mm (¼-in) plain piping nozzle. Pipe rounds 3 cm (1¼ in) in diameter onto the baking tray, spacing them 2–3 cm apart. (The mixture will spread after piping so make the rounds slightly smaller than you want your shells to be.) Tap the tray firmly on the bench a couple of times to knock out any air bubbles.

6. The macaron shells must now stand at room temperature until a crust forms – this will take 2–6 hours, depending on the temperature and humidity of the room. (The warmer and less humid the room, the faster the drying process.) When they are ready you should be able to touch one lightly and have no mixture stick to your finger.

7. Preheat oven to 150°C (300°F).

8. Place macaron shells into the oven and immediately turn the temperature down to 130°C (265°F). Bake for 10–12 minutes, until firm to the touch but not coloured. Remove from the oven and cool completely on the baking tray.

MAKES 60

225 g (8 oz) pure icing sugar
140 g (5 oz) almond meal
100 g (3½ oz) eggs whites, at room temperature

Chocolate
MACARON SHELLS

MAKES 60

225 g (8 oz) pure icing sugar
140 g (5 oz) almond meal
2 tablespoons cocoa
110 g (4 oz) egg whites,
at room temperature

1   Line two baking trays with baking paper or silicon baking mats.

2   Combine the icing sugar, almond meal and cocoa, and sift together twice, discarding anything remaining in the sieve. Set aside.

3   In the bowl of an electric mixer fitted with the whisk attachment, beat the egg whites on high speed until stiff peaks form.

4   Fold the sifted sugar, almond meal and cocoa into the egg whites, continuing to fold until the mixture is glossy and moves slowly when the bowl is tilted.

5   Spoon the mixture into a piping bag fitted with a 5-mm (¼-in) plain piping nozzle. Pipe rounds 3 cm (1¼ in) in diameter onto the baking tray, spacing them 2–3 cm apart. (The mixture will spread after piping so make the rounds slightly smaller than you want your shells to be.) Tap the tray firmly on the bench a couple of times to knock out any air bubbles.

6   The macaron shells must now stand at room temperature until a crust forms – this will take 2–6 hours, depending on the temperature and humidity of the room. (The warmer and less humid the room, the faster the drying process.) When they are ready you should be able to touch one lightly and have no mixture stick to your finger.

7   Preheat oven to 150°C (300 F).

8   Place macaron shells into the oven and immediately turn the temperature down to 130°C (265°F). Bake for 10–12 minutes, until firm to the touch. Remove from the oven and cool completely on the baking tray.

Chamomile Macarons

MAKES 30

FILLING

150 g (5 oz) white chocolate, chopped
120 ml (4 fl oz) pouring cream
1 tablespoon chamomile tea leaves

Melt the chocolate over a double boiler or in the microwave. (If using the microwave, heat the chocolate for 20 seconds at a time, stirring between bursts.)

Pour the cream into a small saucepan and bring to the boil, stir in the chamomile tea leaves and remove from the heat. Stand for 5 minutes. Strain the cream to remove tea leaves, reheat until hot, then pour it over the chocolate and stir until smooth.

Refrigerate the filling for 30 minutes or until firm enough to hold its shape.

Spoon or pipe the filling onto half the macaron shells, then sandwich with the remaining shells.

SHELLS

1 quantity basic macaron shells (p. 10)
1 vanilla bean, split and seeds scraped

Make the macaron shells following the method given, adding the vanilla seeds to the egg whites while beating.

Black Forest Macarons

SHELLS

1 quantity chocolate macaron shells (p. 13)

Make the chocolate macaron shells following the method given.

FILLING

3 egg yolks
1 vanilla bean, split and seeds scraped
90 g (3 oz) caster sugar
2 tablespoons (1½ fl oz) water
125 g (4½ oz) softened unsalted butter, chopped
90 g (3 oz) cherry jam

In the bowl of an electric mixer fitted with the whisk attachment, beat the egg yolks and vanilla seeds on high speed for 10 minutes, until pale and creamy.

Place the sugar and water in a small saucepan and bring to the boil. Insert a sugar thermometer and simmer until the syrup reaches 121°C (250°F).

With the mixer on medium speed, slowly pour the sugar syrup into the creamed yolks. Beat on high speed for 10 minutes, until cool. With the mixer on medium speed, add the softened butter a cube at a time, allowing each piece to mix in before adding the next. Beat on high speed for 2 minutes. Add the cherry jam and beat for another 2 minutes.

Spoon or pipe the filling onto half the macaron shells, then sandwich with the remaining shells.

Almond Praline Macarons

MAKES 30

FILLING

30 g (1 oz) caster sugar
1 tablespoon (¾ fl oz) water
40 g (1½ oz) whole blanched almonds
10 g (⅜ oz) unsalted butter, diced
150 g (5 oz) milk chocolate, chopped
120 ml (4 fl oz) pouring cream

Grease a baking tray.

Combine the sugar and water in a small saucepan and bring to the boil. Add the almonds and cook over medium heat, stirring continuously, until the sugar caramelises and coats the almonds. As soon as the nuts are caramelised, remove pan from the heat and add the butter. Mix well, then spread on the baking tray to cool.

Melt the chocolate over a double boiler or in the microwave. (If using the microwave, heat the chocolate for 20 seconds at a time, stirring between bursts.) Pour the cream into a small saucepan and heat until hot, then pour it over the chocolate and stir until smooth.

Chop the caramelised almonds finely, then stir them into the chocolate ganache filling.

Refrigerate the filling for 30 minutes or until firm enough to hold its shape.

Spoon or pipe the filling onto half the macaron shells, then sandwich with the remaining shells.

SHELLS

1 quantity basic macaron shells (p. 10)

Make the basic macaron shells following the method given.

Blackcurrant and Violet Macarons

SHELLS

1 quantity basic macaron shells (p. 10)
purple food colouring
2 teaspoons crushed crystallised violets

Make the macaron shells following the method given, adding enough purple food colouring to the egg whites to achieve a pale-purple colour. Immediately after piping the shells, sprinkle them with the crushed violets.

FILLING

3 egg yolks
90 g (3 oz) caster sugar
2 tablespoons (1½ fl oz) water
125 g (4½ oz) softened unsalted butter, chopped
60 g (2 oz) blackcurrant jam
½ teaspoon violet extract

In the bowl of an electric mixer fitted with the whisk attachment, beat the egg yolks on high speed for 10 minutes, until pale and creamy.

Place the sugar and water in a small saucepan and bring to the boil, insert a sugar thermometer and simmer until the syrup reaches 121°C (250°F).

With the mixer on medium speed, slowly pour the sugar syrup into the creamed yolks. Beat on high speed for 10 minutes, until cool. With the mixer on medium speed, add the softened butter a cube at a time, allowing each piece to mix in before adding the next. Beat on high speed for 2 minutes. Add the blackcurrant jam and violet extract and beat again for 2 minutes.

Spoon or pipe the filling onto half the macaron shells, then sandwich with the remaining shells.

Chocolate Coconut Macarons

MAKES 30

FILLING

150 g (5 oz) dark chocolate
150 ml (5 fl oz) pouring cream
40 g (1½ oz) desiccated coconut
1 tablespoon (¾ fl oz) coconut liqueur

Melt the chocolate over a double boiler or in the microwave. (If using the microwave, heat the chocolate for 20 seconds at a time, stirring between bursts.) Pour the cream into a small saucepan and heat until hot, pour it over the chocolate and stir until smooth. Add the desiccated coconut and coconut liqueur, and stir until combined.

Refrigerate the filling for 30 minutes or until firm enough to hold its shape.

Spoon or pipe the filling onto half the macaron shells, then sandwich with the remaining shells.

SHELLS

1 quantity chocolate macaron shells (p. 13)
1 tablespoon desiccated coconut

Make the macaron shells following the method given. Immediately after piping the shells, sprinkle with desiccated coconut.

Passionfruit Macarons

SHELLS

1 quantity basic macaron shells (p. 10)
yellow food colouring

Make the macaron shells following the method given, adding enough yellow food colouring to the egg whites to achieve a pale-yellow colour.

FILLING

3 egg yolks
90 g (3 oz) caster sugar
2 tablespoons (1½ fl oz) water
125 g (4½ oz) softened unsalted butter, chopped
60 g (2 oz) passionfruit pulp, unstrained (from about 2 passionfruit)

In the bowl of an electric mixer fitted with the whisk attachment, beat the egg yolks on high speed for 10 minutes, until pale and creamy.

Place the sugar and water in a small saucepan and bring to the boil. Insert a sugar thermometer and simmer until the syrup reaches 121°C (250°F).

With the mixer on medium speed, slowly pour the sugar syrup into the creamed yolks. Beat on high speed for 10 minutes, until cool. With the mixer on medium speed, add the softened butter a cube at a time, allowing each piece to mix in before adding the next. Beat on high speed for 2 minutes. Add the passionfruit pulp and beat on high speed for 2 minutes.

Spoon or pipe the filling onto half the macaron shells, then sandwich with the remaining shells.

Vanilla Rose Macarons

MAKES 30

FILLING

3 egg yolks

1 vanilla bean, split and seeds
  scraped

90 g (3 oz) caster sugar

2 tablespoons (1½ fl oz) water

125 g (4½ oz) softened unsalted
  butter, chopped

½ teaspoon rose extract

In the bowl of an electric mixer fitted with the whisk attachment, beat the egg yolks and vanilla seeds on high speed for 10 minutes, until pale and creamy.

Place the sugar and water in a small saucepan and bring to the boil. Insert a sugar thermometer and simmer until the syrup reaches 121°C (250°F).

With the mixer on medium speed, slowly pour the sugar syrup into the creamed yolks. Beat on high speed for 10 minutes, until cool. With the mixer on medium speed, add the softened butter a cube at a time, allowing each piece to mix in before adding the next. Beat on high speed for 2 minutes. Add the rose extract and beat for 2 minutes.

Spoon or pipe the filling onto half the macaron shells, then sandwich with the remaining shells.

SHELLS

1 quantity basic macaron shells (p. 10)
pink food colouring

Make the macaron shells following the method given, adding enough pink food colouring to the egg whites to achieve a pale-pink colour.

Chocolate *and* Raspberry Macarons

SHELLS

1 quantity basic macaron shells (p. 10)
pink food colouring
2 teaspoons cocoa

Make the macaron shells following
the method given, adding enough pink
food colouring to the egg whites
to achieve a dark-pink colour.
Immediately after piping the shells,
dust them lightly with cocoa.

FILLING

200 g (7 oz) raspberries
150 g (5 oz) dark chocolate, chopped
2 teaspoons raspberry liqueur

Place raspberries in a food processor or blender and purée until smooth, then press through a sieve to remove seeds. Weigh out 150 g (5 oz) of the purée and pour it into a small saucepan. Set aside.

Melt the chocolate over a double boiler or in the microwave. (If using the microwave, heat the chocolate for 20 seconds at a time, stirring between bursts.) Heat the raspberry purée until hot, then pour it over the dark chocolate and stir until smooth. Add the raspberry liqueur and stir until combined.

Refrigerate the filling for 30 minutes or until firm enough to hold its shape.

Spoon or pipe the filling onto half the macaron shells, then sandwich with the remaining shells.

Cinnamon Macarons

MAKES 30

FILLING

150 g (5 oz) milk chocolate, chopped
120 ml (4 fl oz) pouring cream
½ teaspoon ground cinnamon

Melt the chocolate over a double boiler or in the microwave. (If using the microwave, heat the chocolate for 20 seconds at a time, stirring between bursts.) Pour the cream into a small saucepan, add the cinnamon and heat until hot, then pour it over the chocolate and stir until smooth.

Refrigerate the filling for 30 minutes or until firm enough to hold its shape.

Spoon or pipe the filling onto half the macaron shells, then sandwich with the remaining shells.

SHELLS

1 quantity basic macaron shells (p. 10)
1 teaspoon ground cinnamon

Make the macaron shells following the method given. Immediately after piping the shells, sprinkle them lightly with ground cinnamon.

Coconut Macarons

MAKES 30

SHELLS

1 quantity basic macaron shells (p. 10)
2 teaspoons desiccated coconut, toasted

Make the macaron shells following the method given. Immediately after piping the shells, sprinkle them with toasted desiccated coconut.

FILLING

3 egg yolks
90 g (3 oz) caster sugar
2 tablespoons (1½ fl oz) water
125 g (4½ oz) softened unsalted butter, chopped

1 teaspoon vanilla extract
40 g (1½ oz) desiccated coconut, toasted
1½ tablespoons (1 fl oz) coconut liqueur

In the bowl of an electric mixer fitted with the whisk attachment, beat the egg yolks on high speed for 10 minutes, until pale and creamy.

Place the sugar and water in a small saucepan and bring to the boil. Insert a sugar thermometer and simmer until the syrup reaches 121°C (250°F).

With the mixer on medium speed, slowly pour the sugar syrup into the creamed yolks. Beat on high speed for 10 minutes, until cool. With the mixer on medium speed, add the softened butter a cube at a time, allowing each piece to mix in before adding the next. Beat on high speed for 2 minutes. Combine the desiccated coconut and coconut liqueur in a bowl, then add to the buttercream. Beat again for 2 minutes on high speed.

Spoon or pipe the filling onto half the macaron shells, then sandwich with the remaining shells.

Raspberry Macarons

MAKES 30

FILLING

3 egg yolks
1 vanilla bean, split and seeds
    scraped
90 g (3 oz) caster sugar
2 tablespoons (1½ fl oz) water

125 g (4½ oz) softened unsalted
    butter, chopped
90 g (3 oz) raspberry jam
30 fresh raspberries

In the bowl of an electric mixer fitted with the whisk attachment, beat the egg yolks and vanilla seeds on high speed for 10 minutes, until pale and creamy.

Place the sugar and water in a small saucepan and bring to the boil. Insert a sugar thermometer and simmer until the syrup reaches 121°C (250°F).

With the mixer on medium speed, slowly pour the sugar syrup into the creamed yolks. Beat on high speed for 10 minutes, until cool. With the mixer on medium speed, add the softened butter a cube at a time, allowing each piece to mix in before adding the next. Beat on high speed for 2 minutes. Add the raspberry jam and beat for 2 minutes.

Spoon or pipe the filling onto half the macaron shells, put a fresh raspberry in the centre of each, then sandwich with the remaining shells.

SHELLS

1 quantity basic macaron shells (p. 10)
pink food colouring

Make the macaron shells following the method given, adding enough pink food colouring to the egg whites to achieve a dark-pink colour.

Gianduja Macarons

SHELLS

1 quantity basic macaron shells (p. 10)
brown food colouring

Make the macaron shells following the method given, adding enough brown food colouring to the egg whites to achieve a pale-caramel colour.

FILLING

30 g (1 oz) hazelnuts
30 g (1 oz) caster sugar
1 tablespoon (¾ fl oz) water
10 g (⅜ oz) butter

150 g (5 oz) gianduja chocolate, chopped
120 ml (4 fl oz) pouring cream

Preheat oven to 160°C (320°F).

Place the hazelnuts on a baking tray and roast for 5 minutes, until they are nicely toasted and the skins loose. Allow to cool slightly, then rub the hazelnuts between your hands to remove the skins.

Grease a baking tray.

Place the sugar and water in a small saucepan and bring to the boil. Add the peeled hazelnuts and cook over medium heat, stirring continuously, until the sugar caramelises around the hazelnuts. As soon as the nuts are caramelised, remove pan from the heat and add the butter. Mix well, then spread the hazelnuts on the greased baking tray to cool.

Melt the chocolate over a double boiler or in the microwave. (If using the microwave, heat the chocolate for 20 seconds at a time, stirring between bursts.) Pour the cream into a small saucepan and heat until hot, then pour it over the chocolate and stir until smooth.

Refrigerate the filling for 30 minutes or until firm enough to hold its shape.

Spoon or pipe the filling onto half the macaron shells, place a caramelised hazelnut in the centre of each, then sandwich with the remaining shells.

Gingerbread-spiced Macarons

MAKES 30

FILLING

150 g (5 oz) milk chocolate,
    chopped
150 ml (5 fl oz) pouring cream
2 strips orange zest
1 cinnamon stick
1 star anise

1 clove
2 cardamom pods
pinch of freshly grated nutmeg
3 teaspoons honey
½ vanilla bean, split and seeds
    scraped

Melt the chocolate over a double boiler or in the microwave. (If using the microwave, heat the chocolate for 20 seconds at a time, stirring between bursts.) Pour the cream into a small saucepan and add the orange zest, cinnamon, star anise, clove, cardamom, nutmeg, honey, vanilla pod and seeds. Bring to the boil, then remove from the heat and stand for 10 minutes. Strain the cream, then reheat until hot, pour it over the chocolate and stir until smooth.

Refrigerate the filling for 30 minutes or until firm enough to hold its shape.

Spoon or pipe the filling onto half the macaron shells, then sandwich with the remaining shells.

SHELLS

1 quantity basic macaron shells (p. 10)
brown food colouring
½ teaspoon freshly grated nutmeg

Make the macaron shells following the method given, adding enough brown food colouring to the egg whites to achieve a pale-caramel colour. Immediately after piping the shells, sprinkle them with grated nutmeg.

Saffron and Vanilla Macarons

SHELLS

1 quantity basic macaron shells (p. 10)
1 vanilla bean, split and seeds scraped
½ teaspoon saffron powder

Make the macaron shells following the method given, adding the seeds of the vanilla bean to the egg whites while beating. Immediately after piping the shells, sprinkle them with saffron powder.

FILLING

3 egg yolks
1 vanilla bean, split and seeds scraped
90 g (3 oz) caster sugar
2 tablespoons (1½ fl oz) water
125 g (4½ oz) softened unsalted butter, chopped
½ teaspoon saffron powder

In the bowl of an electric mixer fitted with the whisk attachment, beat the egg yolks and vanilla seeds on high speed for 10 minutes, until pale and creamy.

Place the sugar and water in a small saucepan and bring to the boil. Insert a sugar thermometer and simmer until the syrup reaches 121°C (250°F).

With the mixer on medium speed, slowly pour the sugar syrup into the creamed yolks. Beat on high speed for 10 minutes, until cool. With the mixer on medium speed, add the softened butter a cube at a time, allowing each piece to mix in before adding the next. Add the saffron powder and beat on high speed for 2 minutes.

Spoon or pipe the filling onto half the macaron shells, then sandwich with the remaining shells.

Hazelnut Praline Macarons

MAKES 30

FILLING

3 egg yolks
90 g (3 oz) caster sugar
2 tablespoons (1½ fl oz) water
125 g (4½ oz) softened unsalted butter, chopped
60 g (2 oz) hazelnut praline paste

In the bowl of an electric mixer fitted with the whisk attachment, beat the egg yolks on high speed for 10 minutes, until pale and creamy.

Place the sugar and water in a small saucepan and bring to the boil. Insert a sugar thermometer and simmer until the syrup reaches 121°C (250°F).

With the mixer on medium speed, slowly pour the sugar syrup into the creamed yolks. Beat on high speed for 10 minutes, until cool. With the mixer on medium speed, add the softened butter a cube at a time, allowing each piece to mix in before adding the next. Beat on high speed for 2 minutes. Add the hazelnut praline and beat for 2 minutes.

Spoon or pipe the filling onto half the macaron shells, then sandwich with the remaining shells.

SHELLS

1 quantity basic macaron shells (p. 10)
1 vanilla bean, split and seeds scraped

Make the macaron shells following the method given, adding the vanilla seeds to the egg whites while beating.

Honey and Sesame Macarons

SHELLS

1 quantity basic macaron shells (p. 10)
2 teaspoons sesame seeds

Make the macaron shells following the method given. Immediately after piping the shells, sprinkle them with the sesame seeds.

FILLING

3 egg yolks
50 g (1¾ oz) caster sugar
50 g (1¾ oz) honey
2 tablespoons (1½ fl oz) water

125 g (4½ oz) softened unsalted butter, chopped
2 tablespoons sesame seeds, toasted

In the bowl of an electric mixer fitted with the whisk attachment, beat the egg yolks on high speed for 10 minutes, until pale and creamy.

Place the sugar, honey and water in a small saucepan and bring to the boil. Insert a sugar thermometer and simmer until the syrup reaches 121°C (250°F).

With the mixer on medium speed, slowly pour the sugar syrup into the creamed yolks. Beat on high speed for 10 minutes, until cool. With the mixer on medium speed, add the softened butter a cube at a time, allowing each piece to mix in before adding the next. Beat on high speed for 2 minutes. Add the toasted sesame seeds and mix well.

Spoon or pipe the filling onto half the macaron shells, then sandwich with the remaining shells.

Jasmine Tea & Lime Macarons

MAKES 30

FILLING

150 g (5 oz) white chocolate, chopped
120 ml (4 fl oz) pouring cream
1 tablespoon jasmine tea leaves
finely grated zest of 2 limes

Melt the chocolate over a double boiler or in the microwave. (If using the microwave, heat the chocolate for 20 seconds at a time, stirring between bursts.) Pour the cream into a small saucepan and bring to the boil, then remove from the heat and add the jasmine tea and lime zest. Stand for 10 minutes. Strain the cream to remove tea leaves, reheat until hot, then pour it over the chocolate and stir until smooth.

Refrigerate the filling for 30 minutes or until firm enough to hold its shape.

Spoon or pipe the filling onto half the macaron shells, then sandwich with the remaining shells.

SHELLS

1 quantity basic macaron shells (p. 10)
green food colouring
2 teaspoons jasmine tea leaves

Make the macaron shells following the method given, adding enough green food colouring to the egg whites to achieve a pale-lime colour. Immediately after piping the shells, sprinkle them with jasmine tea leaves.

Strawberry, Vanilla *and* Lychee Macarons

SHELLS

1 quantity basic macaron shells (p. 10)
pink food colouring

Make the macaron shells following the method given, adding enough pink food colouring to the egg whites to achieve a pale-pink colour.

FILLING

3 egg yolks
1 vanilla bean, split and seeds scraped
90 g (3 oz) caster sugar
2 tablespoons (1½ fl oz) water

125 g (4½ oz) softened unsalted butter, chopped
90 g (3 oz) strawberry jam
1 × 560-g (1 lb 4 oz) can lychees, drained and cut into 1-cm pieces

In the bowl of an electric mixer fitted with the whisk attachment, beat the egg yolks and vanilla seeds on high speed for 10 minutes, until pale and creamy.

Place the sugar and water in a small saucepan and bring to the boil. Insert a sugar thermometer and simmer until the syrup reaches 121°C (250°F).

With the mixer on medium speed, slowly pour the sugar syrup into the creamed yolks. Beat on high speed for 10 minutes, until cool. With the mixer on medium speed, add the softened butter a cube at a time, allowing each piece to mix in before adding the next. Beat on high speed for 2 minutes. Add the strawberry jam and beat for 2 minutes.

Spoon or pipe the filling onto half the macaron shells. Place a piece of lychee in the centre of each, then sandwich with the remaining shells.

Lime and Coconut Macarons

MAKES 30

FILLING

3 egg yolks
90 g (3 oz) caster sugar
2 tablespoons (1½ fl oz) water
125 g (4½ oz) softened unsalted
   butter, chopped
finely grated zest of 3 limes
30 g (1 oz) desiccated coconut
1 tablespoon (¾ fl oz) coconut
   liqueur

In the bowl of an electric mixer fitted with the whisk attachment, beat the egg yolks on high speed for 10 minutes, until pale and creamy.

Place the sugar and water in a small saucepan and bring to the boil. Insert a sugar thermometer and simmer until the syrup reaches 121°C (250°F).

With the mixer on medium speed, slowly pour the sugar syrup into the creamed yolks. Beat on high speed for 10 minutes, until cool. With the mixer on medium speed, add the softened butter a cube at a time, allowing each piece to mix in before adding the next. Beat on high speed for 2 minutes. Add the lime zest, desiccated coconut and liqueur and beat for 2 minutes.

Spoon or pipe the filling onto half the macaron shells, then sandwich with the remaining shells.

SHELLS

1 quantity basic macaron shells (p. 10)
green food colouring
2 teaspoons desiccated coconut

Make the macaron shells following the method given, adding enough green food colouring to the egg whites to achieve a lime colour. Immediately after piping the shells, sprinkle them with the desiccated coconut.

Liquorice Macarons

SHELLS

1 quantity basic macaron shells (p. 10)
black food colouring

Make the macaron shells following the method given, adding enough black food colouring to the egg whites to achieve a dark-grey colour.

FILLING

150 g (5 oz) white chocolate, chopped
200 ml (7 fl oz) pouring cream
120 g (4 oz) soft liquorice, finely chopped

Melt the chocolate over a double boiler or in the microwave. (If using the microwave, heat the chocolate for 20 seconds at a time, stirring between bursts.) Pour the cream into a small saucepan, add the liquorice and bring to the boil. Remove from heat and use a fork to blend the liquorice into the cream. Pour the hot cream over the chocolate and stir until smooth.

Refrigerate the filling for 30 minutes or until firm enough to hold its shape.

Spoon or pipe the filling onto half the macaron shells, then sandwich with the remaining shells.

White Chocolate and Lavender Macarons

MAKES 30

FILLING

150 g (5 oz) white chocolate
120 ml (4 fl oz) pouring cream
2 teaspoons dried cooking lavender
purple food colouring

Melt the chocolate over a double boiler or in the microwave. (If using the microwave, heat the chocolate for 20 seconds at a time, stirring between bursts.) Pour the cream into a small saucepan and bring to the boil, then add the lavender. Stand for 5 minutes. Strain the cream to remove lavender, then reheat until hot, pour it over the chocolate and stir until smooth. Stir in enough purple food colouring to achieve a pale-purple colour.

Refrigerate the filling for 30 minutes or until firm enough to hold its shape.

Spoon or pipe the filling onto half the macaron shells, then sandwich with the remaining shells.

SHELLS

1 quantity basic macaron shells (p. 10)
1 vanilla bean, split and seeds scraped

Make the macaron shells following the method given, adding the seeds of the vanilla bean to the egg whites while beating.

Mint-chocolate Macarons

SHELLS

1 quantity basic macaron shells (p. 10)
green food colouring
2 teaspoons cocoa (unsweetened)

Make the macaron shells following the method given, adding enough green food colouring to the egg whites to achieve a pale-green colour. Immediately after piping the shells, dust them with cocoa.

FILLING

150 g (5 oz) dark chocolate, chopped
150 ml (5 fl oz) pouring cream
½ cup fresh mint leaves, roughly chopped
½ teaspoon mint essence

Melt the chocolate over a double boiler or in the microwave. (If using the microwave, heat the chocolate for 20 seconds at a time, stirring between bursts.) Pour the cream into a small saucepan and bring to the boil, then remove from the heat and add the mint leaves. Stand for 10 minutes. Strain the cream to remove leaves, then reheat until hot, pour it over the dark chocolate and stir until smooth. Add the mint essence and mix well.

Refrigerate the filling for 30 minutes or until firm enough to hold its shape.

Spoon or pipe the filling onto half the macaron shells, then sandwich with the remaining shells.

Passionfruit and Milk Chocolate Macarons

MAKES 30

FILLING

10–14 passionfruit
150 g (5 oz) milk chocolate, chopped

Cut the passionfruits in half, scoop out the seeds and pulp, and press through a sieve to collect the juice. Discard any seeds or pulp left in the sieve. Measure out 120 ml (4 fl oz) of passionfruit juice and place in a small saucepan. Set aside.

Melt the chocolate over a double boiler or in the microwave. (If using the microwave, heat the chocolate for 20 seconds at a time, stirring between bursts.) Heat the passionfruit juice until hot, then pour it over the chocolate and stir until smooth.

Refrigerate the filling for 30 minutes or until firm enough to hold its shape.

Spoon or pipe the filling onto half the macaron shells, then sandwich with the remaining shells.

SHELLS

1 quantity basic macaron shells (p. 10)
yellow food colouring

Make the macaron shells following the method given, adding enough yellow food colouring to the egg whites to achieve a deep-yellow colour.

Vanilla Macarons

SHELLS

1 quantity basic macaron shells (p. 10)
1 vanilla bean, split and seeds scraped

Make the macaron shells following the method given, adding the seeds of the vanilla bean to the egg whites while beating.

FILLING

3 egg yolks
1 vanilla bean, split and seeds scraped
90 g (3 oz) caster sugar
2 tablespoons (1½ fl oz) water
125 g (4½ oz) softened unsalted butter, chopped

In the bowl of an electric mixer fitted with the whisk attachment, beat the egg yolks and vanilla seeds on high speed for 10 minutes, until pale and creamy.

Place the sugar and water in a small saucepan and bring to the boil. Insert a sugar thermometer and simmer until the syrup reaches 121°C (250°F).

With the mixer on medium speed, slowly pour the sugar syrup into the creamed yolks. Beat on high speed for 10 minutes, until cool. With the mixer on medium speed, add the softened butter a cube at a time, allowing each piece to mix in before adding the next. Beat on high speed for 2 minutes.

Spoon or pipe the filling onto half the macaron shells, then sandwich with the remaining shells.

Chocolate & Orange Macarons

MAKES 30

FILLING

150 ml (5 fl oz) pouring cream
finely grated zest of 2 oranges
150 g (5 oz) dark chocolate, chopped
1 tablespoon (¾ fl oz) orange liqueur

Melt the chocolate over a double boiler or in the microwave. (If using the microwave, heat the chocolate for 20 seconds at a time, stirring between bursts.) Pour the cream into a small saucepan, add the finely grated orange zest and bring to the boil. Stand for 10 minutes. Strain the cream to remove zest, reheat until hot, then pour it over the chocolate and stir until smooth. Add the orange liqueur and mix well.

Refrigerate the filling for 30 minutes or until firm enough to hold its shape.

Spoon or pipe the filling onto half the macaron shells, then sandwich with the remaining shells.

SHELLS

1 quantity basic macaron shells (p. 10)
red food colouring
yellow food colouring
2 teaspoons cocoa

Make the macaron shells following the method given, adding enough red and yellow food colouring to the egg whites to achieve a bright-orange colour. Immediately after piping the shells, dust them lightly with the cocoa.

Peanut Butter Macarons

SHELLS

1 quantity basic macaron shells (p. 10)
brown food colouring
2 teaspoons finely ground roasted
   peanuts

Make the macaron shells following the method given, adding enough brown food colouring to the egg whites to achieve a caramel colour. Immediately after piping the shells, sprinkle them with the finely ground peanuts.

FILLING

3 egg yolks
90 g (3 oz) caster sugar
2 tablespoons (1½ fl oz) water
125 g (4½ oz) softened unsalted
   butter, chopped

100 g (3½ oz) smooth peanut butter
60 g (2 oz) roasted peanuts,
   chopped

In the bowl of an electric mixer fitted with the whisk attachment, beat the egg yolks on high speed for 10 minutes, until pale and creamy.

Place the sugar and water in a small saucepan and bring to the boil. Insert a sugar thermometer and simmer until the syrup reaches 121°C (250°F).

With the mixer on medium speed, slowly pour the sugar syrup into the creamed yolks. Beat on high speed for 10 minutes, until cool. With the mixer on medium speed, add the softened butter a cube at a time, allowing each piece to mix in before adding the next. Beat on high speed for 2 minutes. Add the peanut butter and chopped peanuts and beat for 2 minutes.

Spoon or pipe the filling onto half the macaron shells, then sandwich with the remaining shells.

Pistachio *and* White Chocolate Macarons

MAKES 30

FILLING

150 g (5 oz) white chocolate, chopped
120 ml (4 fl oz) pouring cream
1 tablespoon pistachio paste

Melt the chocolate over a double boiler or in the microwave. (If using the microwave, heat the chocolate for 20 seconds at a time, stirring between bursts.) Pour the cream into a small saucepan and heat until hot, then pour it over the chocolate and stir until smooth. Add the pistachio paste and mix well.

Refrigerate the filling for 30 minutes or until firm enough to hold its shape.

Spoon or pipe the filling onto half the macaron shells, then sandwich with the remaining shells.

SHELLS

1 quantity basic macaron shells (p. 10)
green food colouring

Make the macaron shells following the method given, adding enough green food colouring to the egg whites to achieve a dark-green colour.

Pecan Caramel Macarons

MAKES 30

SHELLS

1 quantity basic macaron
shells (p. 10)
brown food colouring
2 teaspoons finely ground pecan nuts

Make the macaron shells following the method given, adding enough brown food colouring to the egg whites to achieve a caramel colour. Immediately after piping the shells, sprinkle them with finely ground pecans.

FILLING

100 ml (3½ fl oz) pouring cream
190 g (6½ oz) caster sugar
3 egg yolks
2 tablespoons (1½ fl oz) water

125 g (4½ oz) softened unsalted
butter, chopped
60 g (2 oz) pecan nuts, finely
chopped

Pour the cream into a small saucepan and heat until hot. Set aside.

Place 100 g (3½ oz) of the sugar into a medium-sized saucepan and cook over a medium heat, stirring occasionally, until the sugar melts and turns into caramel. Continue to cook the caramel until it is dark golden, then immediately remove from the heat, add the cream and stir to combine. Pour into a bowl and set aside to cool.

In the bowl of an electric mixer fitted with the whisk attachment, beat the egg yolks on high speed for 10 minutes, until pale and creamy.

Place the water and remaining 90 g (3 oz) sugar in a small saucepan and bring to the boil. Insert a sugar thermometer and simmer until the syrup reaches 121°C (250°F).

With the mixer on medium speed, slowly pour the sugar syrup into the creamed yolks. Beat on high speed for 10 minutes, until cool. With the mixer on medium speed, add the softened butter a cube at a time, allowing each piece to mix in before adding the next. Beat on high speed for 2 minutes. Add the cooled caramel and chopped pecans, and beat again for 2 minutes.

Spoon or pipe the filling onto half the macaron shells, then sandwich with the remaining shells.

69

Espresso Macarons

MAKES 30

FILLING

3 teaspoons instant coffee

3 teaspoons hot water

3 egg yolks

90 g (3 oz) caster sugar

2 tablespoons (1½ fl oz) water

125 g (4½ oz) softened unsalted butter, chopped

2 teaspoons vanilla extract

Dissolve the instant coffee in the hot water and set aside to cool.

In the bowl of an electric mixer fitted with the whisk attachment, beat the egg yolks on high speed for 10 minutes, until pale and creamy.

Place the sugar and 2 tablespoons water in a small saucepan and bring to the boil. Insert a sugar thermometer and simmer until the syrup reaches 121°C (250°F).

With the mixer on medium speed, slowly pour the sugar syrup into the creamed yolks. Beat on high speed for 10 minutes, until cool. With the mixer on medium speed, add the softened butter a cube at a time, allowing each piece to mix in before adding the next. Beat on high speed for 2 minutes. Add vanilla extract and cooled coffee to the buttercream, and beat on high speed for 2 minutes.

Spoon or pipe the filling onto half the macaron shells, then sandwich with the remaining shells.

SHELLS

1 quantity basic macaron shells (p. 10)
brown food colouring
2 teaspoons freshly ground coffee

Make the macaron shells following the method given, adding enough brown food colouring to the egg whites to achieve a coffee colour. Immediately after piping the shells, sprinkle them lightly with ground coffee.

Green Tea and Mint Macarons

SHELLS

1 quantity basic macaron shells (p. 10)
green food colouring

Make the macaron shells following the method given, adding enough green food colouring to the egg whites to achieve a pale-green colour.

FILLING

150 g (5 oz) white chocolate, chopped
120 ml (4 fl oz) pouring cream
1 tablespoon green tea leaves
12 fresh mint leaves, roughly chopped

Melt the chocolate over a double boiler or in the microwave. (If using the microwave, heat the chocolate for 20 seconds at a time, stirring between bursts.) Pour the cream into a small saucepan and bring to the boil. Remove from the heat and add the green tea and mint leaves. Stand for 10 minutes. Strain the cream to remove leaves, then reheat until hot, pour it over the chocolate and stir until smooth.

Refrigerate the filling for 30 minutes or until firm enough to hold its shape.

Spoon or pipe the filling onto half the macaron shells, then sandwich with the remaining shells.

Salted-caramel Macarons

MAKES 30

FILLING

100 ml (3½ fl oz) pouring cream
190 g (6½ oz) caster sugar
3 egg yolks
2 tablespoons (1½ fl oz) water

125 g (4½ oz) softened unsalted
  butter, chopped
¼ teaspoon salt

Pour the cream into a small saucepan and heat until hot, then set aside.

Place 100 g (3½ oz) of the sugar in a medium-sized saucepan and cook over a medium heat, stirring occasionally, until the sugar melts and turns into caramel. Continue to cook the caramel until it is dark golden, then immediately remove from the heat, add the cream and stir to combine. Pour into a bowl and set aside to cool.

In the bowl of an electric mixer fitted with the whisk attachment, beat the egg yolks on high speed for 10 minutes, until pale and creamy.

Place the water and remaining 90 g (3 oz) sugar in a small saucepan and bring to the boil. Insert a sugar thermometer and simmer until the syrup reaches 121°C (250°F).

With the mixer on medium speed, slowly pour the sugar syrup into the creamed yolks. Beat on high speed for 10 minutes, until cool. With the mixer on medium speed, add the softened butter a cube at a time, allowing each piece to mix in before adding the next. Beat on high speed for 2 minutes. Add the cooled caramel and the salt, and beat for 2 minutes.

Spoon or pipe the filling onto half the macaron shells, then sandwich with the remaining shells.

SHELLS

1 quantity basic macaron shells (p. 10)
brown food colouring

Make the macaron shells following the method given, adding enough brown food colouring to the egg whites to achieve a pale-caramel colour.

Lemon Macarons

MAKES 30

SHELLS

1 quantity basic macaron
shells (p. 10)
yellow food colouring

Make the macaron shells following the
method given, adding enough yellow
food colouring to the egg whites to
achieve a lemon-yellow colour.

FILLING

juice and zest of 1 lemon
140 g (5 oz) caster sugar
165 g (6 oz) softened unsalted
    butter, chopped

1 egg
3 egg yolks
2 tablespoons (1½ fl oz) water

In a small saucepan, combine the lemon juice and zest, 50 g (1¾ oz) of the sugar and 40 g (1½ oz) of the butter. Stir over a low heat until the sugar has dissolved, then remove from the heat and add the whole egg. Mix well, then return to a low heat and stir continuously until the mixture thickens. Transfer to a bowl, press cling film over the surface of the mixture to prevent a skin forming and refrigerate until cool.

In the bowl of an electric mixer fitted with the whisk attachment, beat the egg yolks on high speed for 10 minutes, until pale and creamy.

Place the water and remaining 90 g (3 oz) sugar in a small saucepan and bring to the boil. Insert a sugar thermometer and simmer until the syrup reaches 121°C (250°F).

With the mixer on medium speed, slowly pour the sugar syrup into the creamed yolks. Beat on high speed for 10 minutes, until cool. With the mixer on medium speed, add the remaining 125 g softened butter a cube at a time, allowing each piece to mix in before adding the next. Beat on high speed for 2 minutes. Add the cooled lemon mixture and beat for 2 minutes.

Spoon or pipe the filling onto half the macaron shells, then sandwich with the remaining shells.

Chocolate Macarons

FILLING

150 g (5 oz) 70% dark chocolate, chopped
150 ml (5 fl oz) pouring cream

Melt the chocolate over a double boiler or in the microwave. (If using the microwave, heat the chocolate for 20 seconds at a time, stirring between bursts.) Pour the cream into a small saucepan and heat until hot, then pour it over the chocolate and stir until smooth.

Refrigerate the filling for 30 minutes or until firm enough to hold its shape.

Spoon or pipe the filling onto half the macaron shells, then sandwich with the remaining shells.

SHELLS

1 quantity chocolate macaron shells (p. 13)

Make the chocolate macaron shells following the method given.

Pistachio, Vanilla and Griottine Macarons

MAKES 30

SHELLS

1 quantity basic macaron shells (p. 10)
1 vanilla bean, split and seeds scraped
2 teaspoons finely chopped pistachios

Make the macaron shells following the method given, adding the vanilla seeds to the egg whites while beating. Immediately after piping the shells, sprinkle them with the chopped pistachios.

FILLING

3 egg yolks
1 vanilla bean, split and seeds scraped
90 g (3 oz) caster sugar
2 tablespoons (1½ fl oz) water
125 g (4½ oz) softened unsalted butter, chopped
1½ tablespoons pistachio paste
30 griottine cherries

In the bowl of an electric mixer fitted with the whisk attachment, beat the egg yolks and vanilla seeds on high speed for 10 minutes, until pale and creamy.

Place the sugar and water in a small saucepan and bring to the boil. Insert a sugar thermometer and simmer until the syrup reaches 121°C (250°F).

With the mixer on medium speed, slowly pour the sugar syrup into the creamed yolks. Beat on high speed for 10 minutes, until cool. With the mixer on medium speed, add the softened butter a cube at a time, allowing each piece to mix in before adding the next. Beat on high speed for 2 minutes. Add the pistachio paste and beat for 2 minutes.

Spoon or pipe the filling onto half the macaron shells and place a griottine cherry in the centre of each, then sandwich with the remaining shells.

Mango & White Chocolate Macarons

MAKES 30

FILLING

1 × 300-g (10½-oz) ripe mango, flesh chopped
150 g (5 oz) white chocolate, chopped

Add mango flesh to a food processor or blender and purée until smooth. Press purée through a sieve, discarding any pulp remaining in sieve. Weigh out 120 g (4 oz) of the mango purée and place it in a small saucepan. Set aside.

Melt the chocolate over a double boiler or in the microwave. (If using the microwave, heat the chocolate for 20 seconds at a time, stirring between bursts.) Heat the mango purée until hot, then pour it over the chocolate and stir until smooth.

Refrigerate the filling for 30 minutes or until firm enough to hold its shape.

Spoon or pipe the filling onto half the macaron shells, then sandwich with the remaining shells.

SHELLS

1 quantity basic macaron shells (p. 10)
yellow food colouring
red food colouring

Make the macaron shells following the method given, adding enough yellow and red food colouring to the egg whites to achieve a pale-orange colour.